A Pocket Guide to Becoming

a Business Wonder Woman

By Kathryn Harris

FCPA, CTA

A Pocket Guide to Becoming a Business Wonder Woman

Kathryn Harris
Office 4C – 61 High Street
WALLAN   VIC   3756

(03) 8657 4919

Kathryn@wonderwoman.business

A Pocket Guide to Becoming a Business Wonder Woman

Office 4C – 61 High Street
Wallan Vic 3756

(03) 8657 4919

Kathryn@wonderwoman.business

ISBN: 978-0-9943742-0-2

Disclaimer

This book contains some great information but it is of a general nature. Make sure you get independent expert advice based on your individual circumstances before making any decisions.

Dedication

This book would never have been possible without the help of the amazing women that surround me.

~ My mum Yvonne, who takes a big load of the child care for my family.

~ My truly incredible staff, past and present, at Harris Business Solutions.

~ And, the two incredible women entrepreneurs who stand by my side:

> Allison LeBusque, fundraiser extraordinaire, my voice of reason and the only woman – other than my doctor – who I've stripped to my undies for.

> Jacqui Brauman, another young female entrepreneur who also happens to be a lawyer and a yoga goddess.

CONTENTS

FOREWARD

Being a business woman is hard, tiring but so rewarding. Many women are juggling so many other responsibilities – children, ageing parents, husbands … the list goes on. We tend to try to be everything to everyone.

Some days I feel like I run two complex businesses. My first involves being a child carer, cleaner, restaurant, taxi, personal assistant, education consultant, nurse, careers advisor and sex worker.

The other involves an accountancy practice.

Women approach business differently to men. Just like we can't stand to urinate (unless we have a she-wee), the way we deal with people and approach problems is not the same. We tend to be more empathetic but we also tend to undersell ourselves and doubt our abilities more. Our other big problem is putting ourselves first because most of us wear so many hats, it's hard to look up from under them.

But by using our natural differences we can actually be better at business than the blokes. We are better at connecting with people and, in business, that can lead to greater success.

This book is designed to help you organise your business journey *before* you begin. It is broken into chapters and contains anecdotes about issues I've faced or that clients and colleagues of mine have encountered. The technical information – the nitty gritty financial and business advice – is provided by me.

This book is written for a female audience. But having said that, the information in it applies to either gender.

I just happen to be of the gender that has breasts.

CHAPTER ONE
PLAN TO DO

Introduction

Don't go into business to create yourself a job. I did this, and although in the long run I have developed a successful business, it isn't the right reason for becoming a business woman.

In 2001, when I was pregnant with child number three, the firm I worked for decided to close their office in our little town and consolidate to their second office in the suburbs of Melbourne. I wasn't prepared to travel with a newborn, a 5 and a 6-year-old, so I twiddled my thumbs for a little while and then started my own business.

It was damn hard juggling babies, toilet training, reading practice, a husband and a growing business. One morning I had to change my outfit because I got weed on as I went out the door to work. Another day

I realised at lunchtime I was wearing one brown shoe and one black shoe.

When I got the call regarding my first quality review from my professional society (a three yearly check of how we accountants do things), I had four children in the office with me. One was quite literally being breastfed, one was on the potty and the other two were supervising the one on the potty. I was on the phone trying to sound professional and in control when my eldest came screaming into my office to tell me the one on the potty has done a poo and then tipped the potty on the floor.

Nothing ruins professionalism like poo!

My start in business didn't involve any planning – I flew by the seat of my pants, usually with one or four kids in tow. I was literally too exhausted and too strung out to manage more than one day at a time. I took in every client who came my way and kept them, regardless of whether they were good, bad or indifferent.

It wasn't the best way to operate a professional firm, although it did give us a distinct family feel as I breastfed a baby while preparing a client's tax return.

Now, 13 years on from hanging out my shingle for the first time, I have a successful business, a fantastic team and an asset that one day I can sell. It's been a long, hard slog but by applying the principles in this book, it does get easier.

This section is to help you establish your business properly, by planning before you hoist your banner and open your doors (unlike I did). It's much easier to do it right at the beginning than trying to patch things up as you go along. This applies equally whether you are starting a business from scratch or purchasing an existing enterprise.

Use this book as your guide. You can refer back to it at any time during your business journey. But remember – it's not the be all and end all and you will still need professional advice before you start, whether buying a business or starting from scratch like I did.

Research

Before you run out to the bank and get yourself an overdraft, do some research. Or lots.

Start with your skill set. What are you good at, what strengths and weaknesses do you have? Out of these skills and strengths, is there anything that can be commercialised?

Just being good at something doesn't mean it will work as a business. Ultimately you want to make a living so the thing you are good at also needs to be wanted or needed by other people, and they need to be willing to pay for it. There needs to be a market for it.

Know your market. For instance, it's probably not a good idea to set up a livestock feed store in an area surrounded by apartment blocks! Is the market oversupplied already? In our small town, we now have more than fifteen take-aways and cafes. Unfortunately there isn't the market to support this many food outlets, and within the next twelve months we will see many disappear.

Is the market too price sensitive? Are there suitable premises in the area or will you have to build?

Investigate the competition. Many large corporations can afford to make it difficult for anyone else to open in their areas, simply because they have the finances to absorb a loss long enough to wait for you to go under.

How long can you manage to support the business until it is established and generating sufficient cash flow? Cash is king and without it, you will struggle to survive. A rule of thumb is to ensure you have enough cash to cover three months of outgoings. It's worth remembering that most small businesses take about five years to become established. Number crunching is essential before you start your business. Many small businesses fail early due to a lack of start-up funds.

All this early research, hard thinking and analysis will stand you in good stead for the next step.

Business planning

"If you fail to plan, you are planning to fail."
  –Benjamin Franklin

Business planning is the second most important thing you can do to give your business a good start.

The most important thing is having a good accountant and business advisor right from the get go.

Another advantage of developing a business plan early on is that it is a very structured process that helps you formalise your ideas. Most business plans have the following sections as a minimum:

- Title page
- Business summary
- About your business
- About your market
- About your future
- About your finances
- Supporting documentation

We'll look at these areas in more detail in the next section, and I've included examples to give you an idea of how they should look and what to include. Your business plan shouldn't be a novel – a simple plan will help you formulate your ideas into something tangible.

For a business plan to be a useful tool it has to be reviewed regularly. Don't just write it and shove it in a drawer or bury it in your hard drive. It has to be a living document that grows and evolves with your business.

Mind you, you don't have to sit down and write it all in one hit. A lot of thought and preparation needs to go into a business plan so remember, *research, review and revise*.

Your business plan explained

This section gives you a blueprint of how to write your business plan. Here I explain the minimum requirements (or sections) that should be included in a business plan, and include an example of how to write each section.

The "Title Page" section of your business plan

This is pretty self-explanatory.

Make sure you keep a record on the title page of when you originally wrote the plan and when it is revised. This makes it easy to see at a glance how the plan is evolving.

Also, you should include all the people who have had input into the plan – and make sure they also have the latest copy.

A Pocket Guide to Becoming a Business Wonder Woman

Example Title Page

Business Plan for

Widgets and Wodgets Transport

75 Tootle Street
LOCOTOWN   VIC   3000

Prepared – 20 February 2014
Revision 1 – 30 April 2014

Prepared by Penny Green and Judy Thumb

Contributions by Allison LeBusque, CPA

The "Business Plan Summary" section of your business plan

This is exactly what it sounds like – a summary of the business plan. This should be concise and contain your business goals, market, and finances.

Basically, it's a summary section within the business plan and although it is the second page of the plan, it will be the last thing you complete.

Example Business Plan Summary

The plan is to operate as a truck owner/driver subcontracting to other transport companies and towing their trailers.

A minimum of eight hours per day for five days per week is to be expected.

The fee for truck and driver is $80 per hour.

There is a high demand for owner-driver trucks in the area.

The strategy to achieve this is to use a second-hand truck, which is to be purchased via bank loan, and use existing contacts in the industry to obtain work.

To help mitigate any potential cash-flow problems from the owner being unable to drive, as identified in the "threats" section of this plan, the business will take out business continuity insurance.

The "About Your Business" section of your business plan

This is where you tell the world what your business is – what it does, where it does it, how it does it and who does it.

Use this section to articulate your passion, but also to be honest about your strengths and weaknesses. Working out what you are good at and what you're not so good at is a very important part of the business planning process. Why? So you can find other people to fill the gaps in your own skills.

There are numerous tools to help you work out what your strengths and weaknesses are. The easiest and least scientific is to draw up two columns on a piece of paper – one for strengths the other for weaknesses.

For strengths consider the following:

- What do I do better than others?
- What are the best parts of my personality?
- What do others say I'm good at?

- What resources can I access?
- Do I have a good support network?

For weaknesses (or in a better way to classify them, "areas to improve") consider the following:

- What skills can you improve?
- What are the worst parts of your personality?
- What resources are you lacking?

The biggest trick with strength and weakness analysis is making sure you are honest and objective with yourself. Self assessment isn't easy and it may be helpful to have a trusted friend or advisor have a look over your list.

Example "About Your Business" (or "Business Profile") section

The business will provide a truck and driver to transport companies to haul their trailers.

The business will be established in central Victoria in the large regional centre of Locotown.

Strengths

The operator has many years working as a truck driver in the industry so is comfortable with the expectations of the job.

There is currently a shortage of appropriately qualified owner-drivers.

Weaknesses

The operator has no fixed-term commitment or contracts in place as yet.

The "About the Market" section of your business plan

This is where you explain who is going to buy your goods and/or services. Every business needs customers – without them, you don't have a business!

Research is important. You need to consider what opportunities and threats exist in the area where your business will operate. For some this may be their local area. For others it may be the World Wide Web.

Opportunities are the areas your business can take advantage of, and threats those that may cause your business to unravel. Opportunities and threats may both be in the same types of information. For instance, they can include population, demographics, availability of space to operate in, competitors, the market's price sensitivity, the availability of appropriate staff, government regulation, change in governments, or transport opportunities. The list is practically endless.

Again, this is about being honest and objective, and another set of eyes may be helpful.

Example Market Profile (or About the Market)

Locotown is in a central position to many major freeways that cross the nation. This has made it a hub for transport companies to operate from.

Opportunities

The operator has the opportunity at a later time to purchase a trailer and therefore increase the earning capacity of the business.

The operator has the opportunity to source work elsewhere if there is availability or the rates are higher.

Threats

The transport market is fairly competitive with new operators entering constantly. This could result in a lowering of rates.

If the driver is unwell or the truck breaks down, there will be no income generated by the business.

The "About the Future" section of your business plan

Where are you heading? What to do you want to be doing with your business in two, five or 10 years?

This section is where you can be a little more creative. It articulates the extension of your dreams and hopes, but has a firm foothold in reality.

Take the planning you've done in previous sections and extend it out to show what the business can do with your strengths and the opportunities in the market. Show how you've overcome those weaknesses and threats, and demonstrate how you will become a viable, growing business.

This section will also include your exit strategy, which we'll discuss further in a later chapter. Obviously you don't want to work forever so how do you plan to translate your valuable business asset into money in your pocket and swan off over the horizon to the next business venture, or retirement?

Example About the Future (or Future Plans)

As previously stated, there is an opportunity for expansion by purchasing a trailer within the next 12 months.

Over the next five years the business will be looking to add a second truck and trailer, and employ a driver. This will help ensure continuity of income, providing at least one truck is operational.

As part of the planning process and once a second truck is operating, the business will pay any profit made by the second truck into a compliant superannuation fund for the owner, to the maximum allowed by legislation.

Based on the profit and loss projection and adding back depreciation, this should be approximately $8,000 per annum towards the owner's retirement.

It is considered that the business will operate for 15 years as a full-time occupation. At that point both trucks will be sold and the owner will be looking to obtain part-time paid employment as a transition to retirement.

The "About your Finances" section of your business plan

This section is where you crunch the numbers, and again your research from earlier is important.

Most business plans as a bare minimum will include a cash-flow forecast for the next 12 months. While this is a forecast and based on estimates, it can't be figures just pulled out of a hat. You need to have a clear idea of how much you will sell each month for the first twelve months, and what your expenses will be.

You also need to include in the cash-flow forecast money you contribute and finance you obtain. It will also include taxes, both sales tax such as Goods and Services Tax (GST), and income tax.

Again your research will be incredibly helpful in this section. By the time you get to here you should know your market, your costs and your selling price.

The other person who you should definitely involve in this section is your accountant.

Example About your Finances (or Financial Position)

Financial Position

Cash-flow projection

	Pre start up	Jun-11	Jul-11	Aug-11	Sep-11	Oct-11	Nov-11	Dec-11	Jan-12	Feb-12	Mar-12	Apr-12	May-12
Cash on hand	$3,000	$3,500	$2,434	$4,014	$5,594	$6,794	$7,671	$8,371	$5,371	$2,751	$618	$1,818	$2,695
Cash receipts													
Payment received			$12,800	$12,800	$12,800	$12,800	$12,800	$12,800	$9,600	$9,600	$12,800	$12,800	$12,800
BAS refund		$3,444											
Loan / other capital injected	$50,000												
Total cash receipts	$50,000	$3,444	$12,800	$12,800	$12,800	$12,800	$12,800	$12,800	$9,600	$9,600	$12,800	$12,800	$12,800
Cash paid out													
Registration					$380			$380			$380		
Repairs and maintenance		$300	$370	$300	$300	$300	$300	$1,300	$300	$300	$300	$300	$1,300
Advertising													
Fuel		$4,333	$4,333	$4,333	$4,333	$4,333	$4,333	$4,333	$4,333	$4,333	$4,333	$4,333	$4,333
Accounting		$580					$880						
Telephone		$100	$140	$140	$140	$140	$140	$140	$140	$140	$140	$140	$140
Insurance		$217	$217	$217	$217	$217	$217	$217	$217	$217	$217	$217	$217
BAS payment						$703				$513		$703	$703
Interest			$367	$362	$357	$352	$347	$342	$336	$332	$326	$321	$316
Subtotal	$0	$5,530	$5,357	$5,352	$6,727	$6,045	$6,717	$6,912	$5,326	$5,835	$3,696	$6,014	$7,009
Loan principal repayment		$1,030	$655	$660	$673	$678	$683	$688	$694	$698	$704	$709	$714
Capital purchase	$49,900												
Owner's withdrawal			$5,200	$5,200	$5,200	$5,200	$5,200	$5,200	$6,200	$6,200	$6,200	$5,200	$5,200
Total cash paid	$49,900	$6,530	$11,220	$11,220	$11,600	$11,928	$12,100	$15,800	$12,220	$11,733	$11,600	$11,928	$13,123
Cash position (end of month)	$3,500	$2,434	$4,014	$5,594	$4,794	$7,671	$8,371	$5,371	$2,751	$618	$1,818	$2,695	$2,372

Profit and loss

**Please note – the following profit and loss is prepared based on a calendar year from business commencement.

Income		
Gross receipts	122 182	
Rebates	4 940	
Total income		127 122
Deductions		
Repairs and maintenance	5 455	
Fuel	47 269	
Registration	1 036	
Accounting	1 300	
Telephone	1 491	
Insurance	2 367	
Interest	3 758	
Depreciation	6 750	
Total deductions		69 426
Net business income		57 696

The "Supporting stuff" section

Just like any good detective, you need to have evidence to support your claims. For your business plan to be considered a legitimate, thought-out process, in this section you need to include how you did your research.

You can also refer to your qualifications, personal assets, statistics and any other information that will back up the facts in your plan.

There is no need for an example section here – you know what to do.

CHAPTER TWO
SET UP FOR SUCCESS

Getting your business set up correctly from day one makes it easier to grow and control. There are many different legal entities through which you can run a business and each has different tax and legal ramifications.

Regardless of how you set up your business, start keeping records from day one in a good, easy-to-use, clear system. Not only is this important when dealing with government authorities, it is important for managing your business.

Structure

How will you set your business up? Is it just you, you and a mate, you and your spouse, or you and the whole damn family? Are you operating just in your state, or are you operating nation-wide or world-wide? Is the business going to run while you work full or part time?

There a lots of things to consider when thinking about how to structure your business and again, this is an area where it is essential to get the right advice as doing it wrong can be costly. Trust me!

In this section we'll go over the most common structures for businesses. This is not a comprehensive list, just what are the most likely options and their benefits and flaws.

Obviously I can't tell you which structure is best for you – this is where your accountant comes in. Make sure you discuss with them what they think is the best way for you to set up.

Sole trader

A sole trader is just that – you on your lonesome. It is the easiest and cheapest structure to set up as it already exists. You're it!

Being on your own, there is no need for agreements, share structures or profit divisions, and the business is all yours.

The downside of this is that any debts are on you personally. If your business can't pay its debts as a sole trader, the people your business owes money to can take your assets – your house, your savings, your car, your grandmother's antique sideboard that she left to you in her will. Obviously they can't just walk into your house and take them, but through the legal system they have a right to your personal assets, not just the business assets.

Tax is entirely on you too. You can't share your profit or leave it in the business to be taxed at a lower rate. The profit for a sole trader is added to any other income you have and taxed at your marginal rate.

The biggest upside of being a sole trader is that it's all yours. You get to make the decisions, you get to reap the rewards. But it is important to have a good support network as sometimes it can be lonely being the one making all the decisions.

It's also important to have adequate insurance as you won't be covered by your state's work cover in most instances.

Partnership

So you and your BFF have a great idea for a business. You've done the research, prepared a plan and are ready to get started. You are a partnership.

A partnership is when you and one or more other individuals or companies, decide to run a business together. It isn't a separate entity – it's each of you as a person running a business collaboratively.

From a legal point of view, a partnership is very like a sole trader – each of you is personally liable for all the debts of the business unless you have an agreement that says otherwise.

This is why it is incredibly important to have a partnership agreement prepared and in place. It doesn't matter how much you love your BFF / spouse / sister / neighbour / whoever – things don't always go to plan. The importance of a partnership agreement is that it sets down what to do when things go wrong or you can't agree. After all, as we know, s**t happens.

My business is now operated through a partnership with Allison LeBusque – another CPA and a woman I consider as my sister from another mother. Most of the time, we get along well. She balances my impetuousness and constant hunger to implement new technology, and I balance her need to see the good in everyone. However, we had to make sure that if we couldn't agree on something, we had a process to sort it out. In our case it involves an independent third party getting involved. It hasn't happened yet but we have the contingency plan in place in case it does.

The other thing our partnership agreement covers is what happens if one of us has had enough and wants out. This could be catastrophic to the party that wants to continue so our agreement states that if I say to

Allison; "I've had enough, buy me out", she immediately has the option to say "nope, you have to buy me out". This way neither of us can pull the pin on the other.

I have seen lots of cases where partnerships go wrong. Our business has dealt with one case recently that involved a father and son. Dad thought the son was paying the Goods and Services Tax (GST) to the Australian Tax Office (ATO) – turns out he wasn't. Unfortunately there was no partnership agreement so now the father has to pay the ATO the full debt as junior has skipped town.

Another issue with partnerships is that it can be difficult to grow and bring new capital into the business. When a partner leaves or a new person comes into the business, a change in entity is needed as well as new agreements and registrations.

Company

A company is like a whole other person, literally. Unlike the previous two structures, companies are separate legal entities. They are not you – they are a separate being that you own. What this means is that all assets and debts belong to the company, not you.

If your business can't pay its debts, the people the business owes money to cannot access your personal assets. There are some exceptions – Pay As You Go (PAYG) withholding and superannuation are two debts the tax office can personally come after you for. This includes amounts for yourself as an employee of your business. Most of the time when a company enters into a finance arrangement the business providing the credit will ask for a director's guarantee. This means that the director of the company, the person in charge (which will usually be you), will agree to pay the debt personally if the company can't.

Setting up and running a company has a lot more costs and obligations attached than being a sole trader or partnership. Companies in Australia are regulated by the Corporations Act 2001. The body that enforces all these regulations is the Australian Securities and Investment Commission, better known as ASIC.

Being a director of a company comes with responsibilities. One of the biggest ones is to ensure the company doesn't trade insolvent. Being insolvent means the business can't pay its debts when they are due. In other words, there isn't enough money or equipment or stock that can be sold to cover the debts the company has. In accounting speak this is negative net assets – less assets than liabilities.

Directors also have a fiduciary[1] duty to act in the best interests of their shareholders. What this means is that you have to make sure you don't do anything deliberately that can devalue the business, and that you don't use the company assets for your own means. This is a sticky area in small business because usually the shareholders and directors are one and the same.

The most important thing to remember when operating through a company is that it isn't your money, car, equipment or cash.

---

[1] A legal duty to act solely in another party's interests. Parties owing this duty are called fiduciaries. The individuals to whom they owe a duty are called principals.

If you do take money out of the business you will usually need to process it as income to yourself in one of two ways – either as an employee receiving a wage that includes a director's fee, or as a dividend. Dividends can be franked if the company has paid tax. This means you will get a tax credit personally equal to the amount of tax paid. Or the dividends can be unfranked.

Adding new people into a company requires issuing shares to them. If you are going to borrow money from the company or invest in the company it is really important that a related party loan document is drawn up.

In Australia we have Division 7A regulations that control how money borrowed from a company by shareholders and their associates is treated. Basically, if you take money out of the company or put your personal expenses through the company bank account, you can end up owing the company money. This is just the same as owing your next door neighbour money, remembering it wasn't your money you spent in the first place. This money has to be paid back, with interest, within a certain time frame or the ATO can make it taxable to you personally. If there is no loan document it has to be paid back before the end of the financial year.

The best advice I can give anyone running their business through a company is to ensure you set up a separate bank account for the company, pay yourself a wage from the company, and don't put any personal expenses through the company bank account. And *always* treat the company as a separate person.

Trust

Trusts are very old common-law structures. A trust is an entity that is looking after things for the people who will eventually benefit. If I gave you $10 and asked you to look after it until my youngest child is 12, we would have set up a very simple trust. You would be the trustee and Ben, my youngest child, would be the beneficiary.

Obviously most trusts are more complicated than the above example. There are two main types of trusts used in Australia – fixed and discretionary.

The beneficiaries in a fixed trust have set rights to assets and income. In a discretionary trust, it is up to the trustee how things get split.

Most of you will have heard of a family trust. This is a discretionary trust that is based around family members. Most standard deeds have an individual as the named beneficiary and then their family as other potential beneficiaries.

My family trust beneficiaries are ordered like this:

- Kathryn Harris
- Her spouse – current or former
- Her children
- Her grandchildren
- Her parents
- Her siblings
- Her spouse's parents
- Her spouse's siblings
- And anyone the trustee nominates

So as you can see, I can have whoever is nominated by the trustee – which in this case is a company that I am the director of. A family trust can be very broad and usually the deed gives the trustee discretion to split both income and assets however they please.

This all sounds great in theory – share the income and tax burden around. But as per usual, the ATO doesn't see it that way and there are numerous rules to limit any tax benefits that are gained from sharing income. A big one is that minors can only have about $400 in "unearned" or "passive" income – that is income that isn't from working, like interest and trust distributions – before they are taxed at penalty (much higher) rates.

Discretionary trusts provide more flexibility for including family members in the business and for tax planning than most other entities.

A unit trust is a fixed trust. Similar to a company in which the owners are shareholders, each person holds units in the trust and according to the deed each individual will have a right to income and assets in line with the amount of units they hold.

This can be a great structure for people who aren't related through which to operate a business. It's also useful when there is property owned in the business.

The units can be owned by individuals, discretionary trusts, companies and even self-managed super funds. While it doesn't have the flexibility of a discretionary trust, it has clear definitions as to who gets what.

Record keeping

We've already covered one type of record you should keep in your business – a business plan. Another important one is financial records. These are made up of bank statements, receipts, invoices, contracts, payroll and agreements.

There are so many fantastic apps to help you keep your business records under control. Gone are the days of Excel spreadsheets and shoe boxes.

Most tax systems insist you keep your business source documents for at least five years. This used to mean filing cabinets and archive boxes full of paper, a lot of which faded to the point of being illegible. Nowadays you can take a photo with your smart phone and upload it straight into your accounting system to store it against the transaction from your bank. The original can go in the shredder or the fire drum.

A solid financial record-keeping system has to include a regularly reconciled bank account. Reconciling means you make sure every dollar that goes into and out of your bank account is recorded in your accounting system. With modern computerised systems this is really easy as most of them import your bank transactions for you. Then you just have to process the transaction by categorising it.

If you are still using a manual system this means checking that the cash receipts into your bank account and the cash payments out of your bank account as recorded in your cash books match up to the balance in your bank account.

While it is still perfectly allowable to keep a manual financial record keeping system, it doesn't make sound business sense. A good computerised system is less time consuming and can provide you with so much more information for decision making. Want to see where your profit is at? Easy – run a profit and loss report. What about how many days it takes people to pay you on average? Or comparing your actual sales and expenses to what you budgeted?

It also makes it much easier to work with your accountant.

Let's look at how accountants deal with a manual system – here's an example.

Sarah Sunny and her husband run a beef cattle and sheep farm in north-east Victoria through a family trust. They have about 150 head of cattle and 320 head of sheep. Each month when Sarah gets her bank statements, she sits down and writes up her cash payments book, ensuring every dollar that has gone out of the bank account is included in the book, the GST recorded and the net put in the appropriate column for categorisation. She does the same for her cash receipts.

At the end of the quarter she prepares the Business Activity Statement (BAS) using the GST columns in her cash receipts and payments book. She does the BAS through the ATO business portal because the ATO no longer issues paper statements. At the end of the year she snail mails the cash receipts and payments books, bank statements, inventory details of livestock,

and any equipment purchases and finance agreements
to their accountant.

The accountant's receptionist receives the package.
She opens it, notes down in their system what they
have received, scans into the firm's document storage
system the bank statements, agreements and what not.
She then passes the package on to the partner in
charge of workflow who allocates it to the accountant
to do the data entry work. The accountant gets started.
She can see that Sarah has reconciled the bank
statements (thank heavens!) so she prepares a
spreadsheet that breaks the income and expenses for
the cash books into months, and reconciles the GST
to the BAS. She then needs to enter this into the firm's
accounting system that allows them to produce the
financial reports – profit and loss, income statement,
balance sheet, depreciation schedule and beneficiary
current accounts.

As she is working through the cash book she sees
some transactions that she is not sure Sarah has
categorised correctly, and some that she has put in
miscellaneous (a category accountants don't believe
in!) so she sends Sarah an email asking for the original

documents. Sarah isn't good at scanning so she mails the documents back. The accountant reviews them, makes the necessary adjustments in her system and produces the reports and tax returns. These are then sent back to Sarah and her husband, with all the original source documents for them to review and sign. The originals are then mailed back to the accountant so that the tax returns can be lodged.

The accountant also sends a big fat bill.

What a long and drawn-out process! It basically involves the accountant re-entering data into a different format to produce reports on information that by this time might be four months old.

The benefit to Sarah and her husband? Not a lot, other than complying with tax law. Although the accountant will be applying tax knowledge, which is worth paying for, a lot of what is going on is historical data entry – not a lot of skill being applied. Yet Sarah still has to pay.

But what if Sarah had a cloud-based computerised system? Picture this alternate scenario.

Molly Moon and her partner have a beef and cattle property next door to Sarah. Their business is very similar – about 160 head of beef cattle and around 310 of sheep. Molly uses a cloud-based accounting system to keep the farm records. This system links directly to her bank account and each night downloads any new transactions.

Being a farmer, Molly gets up early. She makes her cuppa and toast then sits at the kitchen table with her iPad and categorises yesterday's bank transactions. It usually takes her about three minutes. She then has a look at the bills due to be paid in the coming weeks and the invoices that haven't been paid. She sees that Sarah and her husband still haven't paid for the sire services the Moon's bull provided to some of the Sunny's herd. So she emails a statement straight out of her system attached to a reminder email.

Later that day, while Molly is waiting at the bus stop for her kids to get home from school, she starts to think about what would happen if they decrease their sheep numbers by 50 head and increase cattle by 20. She opens up a "what if" generator program in her browser on her iPad, which links to her accounting software that her accountant set up. Using simple slider buttons she adjusts the figures and can see that their profit margin is better on beef cattle than on sheep. Thinking about how they can implement this change, she realises she will need a bigger cattle truck to cope with more animals. She contacts her bank to discuss finance. They want current reports from her accountant as well as predicted cash flow.

Molly calls her accountant to discuss it. The accountant logs into Molly's accounting system while they are chatting. She runs some reports, has a look at the "what if" generator, and uses another app to generate the next twelve months' cash flow based on the increase in beef cattle. She also has a chat to Molly about the tax implications of financing the truck and what might be the most effective way to do it. The accountant tells Molly she'll tidy the reports and have them to the bank by the next afternoon.

Fast forward to the end of the year and the accountant contacts Molly to let her know they are working on her financial records. Molly has uploaded all the source documents into her system, attaching them to transactions where appropriate and storing them in the document library if they are more general documents like the inventory reports. The accountant has very little data entry to do.

Because Molly is on a live cloud system they have already done interims and tax planning so when Molly and her partner receive the reports and tax returns in an email there are no surprises.

So, what's different about these two scenarios?

Molly has up-to-date information that allows her to make strategic decisions about her business. It also lets her collaborate with her accountant in a much more proactive way, making them a far more valuable advisor and taking the sting out of their cost.

What if you're not tech savvy? You have two options – learn or outsource. There are lots of great bookkeepers out there who can be invaluable to your business. The thing to remember is to work with them and actually use the information they are providing.

CHAPTER THREE
PEOPLE WHO NEED PEOPLE

As Babs sang: "People who need people are the luckiest people in the world ..."[2]

We humans work better in groups and to be successful, it is important you surround yourself with people that fill the gaps in your skill set and who support your vision.

There's a great book I love called *Hardwired Humans* by Andrew O'Keeffe, a book that talks about why we behave how we behave based on Jane Goodall's study of chimpanzees. It's a fascinating read but also gives you lots of ideas on how we can modify our behaviour to get the best out of those around us.

Dealing with people, for me, is one of the most rewarding *and* one of the most frustrating aspects of

---

[2] As sung by Barbra Streisand for *Funny Girl*. Music by Jane Styne, lyrics by Bob Merrill, 1964.

being in business. Sometimes I feel like I'm herding cats – all of them heading in different directions. Other times, it all clicks and things seem seamless.

In this chapter we look at three different categories of people that will be involved in your business:

- Employees
- Consultants
- Customers

Employees

Not every business will have employees but as your business grows it's almost certain there will come a time when you need another pair of hands.

Employing staff is tough. The first step Allison and I take is to work out exactly what skills the employee will need to bring to the job. We then work out how easy it would be to teach them those skills if they don't already have them. Most people can be trained to complete tasks, but it is far more difficult to change their personality. You need to make sure your employees are the right fit for your business culture, which is where personality comes in. This means finding out about their values, morals and interests. But it's not so easy to do that in a half-hour interview!

To find employees that have the right fit, you actually need to do some self-examination. What are *your* values, morals and interests? What sort of culture are *you* trying to build in your organisation? What sort of interactions do *you* have with your customers? And do they have a high level of trust in *you*, so much so that you need your staff to display the same traits?

The wrong employee can cost your business if they can't communicate in the right way with – or convey your business principles to – your customers.

When we interview potential staff we make it informal and casual. Allison and I talk about ourselves, our journey, and how we do things. We then discuss the candidate's hopes, how they've dealt with certain situations in previous jobs, and what they want to achieve through working with us.

At the end of the day our hiring decision is made mainly on how we personally relate to the candidate. Most of the time this has worked for us, but we have made a few mistakes.

We've all heard the saying "you pay peanuts, you get monkeys" and this is mostly true. However, it doesn't always have to be about money. As humans, there are many other things we value. For our staff, who aren't the highest paid in the industry, it's about working close to home, having flexibility to be with their children when needed, gaining an extra week's holiday a year and simply being valued.

It's amazing how much an unassuming thank you and some empathy when things aren't going well outside of work can make to an employee's morale.

It's important to give staff feedback, good and bad. Usually when I'm herding cats it's because I haven't been clear on how my staff are performing and what I need from them.

Giving negative feedback is hard but it is necessary and the best way to do it is in an honest and empathetic manner. After all we're all human and we all make mistakes – even me!

Make mistakes a learning experience and together with your staff, consider what could have been done to improve the situation. Most importantly, give negative feedback in a dignified manner. Humiliating people is rarely a good method, no matter how frustrated and angry you may be.

Sometimes all the coaching, feedback and discipline – if it comes to that – can't make an employee the right fit. Other times, changes in business conditions mean that a staff member is no longer required. It's never easy to take away someone's job. Once you have made the decision, rip the BandAid off quickly and let your employee know ASAP. If it is a behavioural issue, make sure you have followed due process by giving warnings and by trying to rectify the situation. If you need to make an employee redundant, again make sure you follow due process and pay any entitlements. As hard as it is, it's worse if you let it fester.

There are lots of legal obligations that come with being an employer. You must keep accurate payroll records, you have to ensure you keep track of leave accrued and taken, you need to ensure you pay the superannuation guarantee (currently 9.5%) and you must provide your staff with a payslip within 24 hours of paying them. More information can be found on the Fair Work website.

Consultants

From time to time you'll also need help from people external to your business, your accountant being one. You might also at varying stages of your business use all sorts of different consultants and trades people.

Just like with permanent employees, it's important to find the right consultant to work with. Some relationships will be of less importance than others but the most important thing to remember is that they are all people – you get back what you give.

It's especially important to have a relationship built on trust and honesty with those who will have access to your business premises and records. It has to go both ways – we don't like clients that aren't honest with us or don't respect our opinion, and as a business person, I suspect you feel the same.

Just like for employees, it's perfectly acceptable to have an interview process for key consultants such as an accountant. Again, have a think about your values and the skills you need in your consultant. Look to build long-term relationships – the "getting to know you and your business" bit is a hard slog but it's worth it to find the right person for the job.

Obviously, people and circumstances change and external consultants are businesses too so they may come and go. You don't have to be sold to any new business owner if your consultant's business changes hands, but remember that if you have had a good relationship with the consultant, it is only fair to give the new owner a go.

Remember in a consultant arrangement you are the customer – think about how you want your customers to be treated and how you'd like them to treat you. Mutual respect is always a winner in these situations.

Customers

The last category of people are your customers. Without customers or clients or patrons – however you want to refer to them – you have no business. It's important to keep customer satisfaction in the forefront of everything you do.

But you also need to think about your own business and the kinds of clients it wants.

When I first started, I took in all clients – no vetting at all. Some were horrid people who had no respect for anything or anyone, and getting paid was often more stressful than what it was worth. I desperately wanted to build my business and I didn't put a lot of thought into the sort of people I wanted to deal with. This came back to bite me as I often procrastinated about doing the work of the clients I didn't feel any connection with. I found that the least worthwhile clients, in terms of monetary value and professional satisfaction, were often the most vocal and needy.

It is very important to work out the sort of people you want to deal with. Again, think about your values and interests. A large part of customer service is in the relationship you build. If you don't like someone, or their view and opinions are completely opposite to yours, you will have trouble dealing with them on a professional level.

In retail environments this can be more difficult to control but it is essential you build a marketing plan that helps you define your customer base and how to sell to them. A good marketing and communications consultant can be very helpful here.

A bad review on social media can quickly undo all the goodwill you've built up. It is worthwhile having procedures in place to deal with unhappy customers. But remember we are all human – sometimes mistakes happen and the best way to deal with them is quickly and honestly. Sometimes saying "I messed up" is the best way to deal with a situation.

The cost of obtaining a new customer can be five to six times that of marketing to an existing customer. It's always worthwhile keeping in contact with your existing customers and being aware of the extra services or products you may be able to offer them.

It's a good idea to keep the *Paretos Principle* in mind –
80% of your income will come from 20% of your
clients. And the same applies to complaints!

CHAPTER FOUR
DEATH AND TAXES

As the saying goes, nothing in life is certain except death and taxes. The purpose of this chapter is to help you plan for both eventualities.

Taxes

"The hardest thing in the world to understand is the income tax."
-    Albert Einstein

Taxes are complex and in Australia they only seem to get messier every time the government tries to simplify them.

I'll begin this chapter by stressing one thing – get a good accountant.

A "good accountant" is one that not only understands business but that also has solid tax accounting knowledge. While nobody should want to cheat on their taxes, nobody wants to pay more than they absolutely have to either.

In Australia, we get taxed at the federal level for income tax, consumption tax (GST) and import duties. State governments levy stamp duties and payroll tax, although technically they can levy income taxes too if they feel the urge. But I think they would be hung, drawn and quartered if they tried!

As a business you will almost certainly have to deal with income tax and GST. If you set up a trust or purchase property or a car, you will have to deal with stamp duty. If your annual payroll in your business is greater than $550,000 per annum (in Victoria – other states may differ) you will have to pay payroll tax.

At the moment the Australian Taxation Office (ATO) regulates and collects income tax and GST and each state's revenue office handles stamp duty and payroll taxes. Even within these organisations it is different areas that handle each type of tax.

The ATO keeps two types of accounts for a business – its Income Tax Account (ITA) and its Integrated Client Account (ICA). The ICA is for Goods and Services Tax (GST), Pay As You Go (PAYG) withholding and PAYG instalments. The ITA arises when an income tax return is lodged and assessed.

The two are completely separate and if you make a payment to the wrong one the ATO won't even realise. They will hound you for a debt you've paid because the debt collection departments can't put the two together. We have actually seen them refund a credit from an ICA when there was an income tax debt of the same amount. It's absolutely ludicrous and totally frustrating for the tax payer!

All Australian business must register for an ABN – an Australian Business Number. The details for this registration are open to the public through the Australian Business Register. This is because if you provide goods or services to someone and don't give them your ABN, they are supposed to keep 49% of the payment and give it straight to the ATO because, obviously, you are a tax cheat! There are some exceptions to this – a person can be operating a hobby or leisure activity and not a business. If this is the case then they can give the purchaser a Statement by Supplier to explain why they don't have an ABN.

You can only have an ABN if you really are a business. One area that is scrutinised for ABNs is labour hire. This is because if all a person is supplying is labour, then they probably should be an employee and therefore don't need an ABN.

So now you have an ABN, do you need to register for GST? If your business gets more than $75,000 in customer payments then you will have to register for GST. If the figure is under that, it's optional, and probably not worth the hassle. Who wants to fill in an extra form (a Business Activity Statement or BAS) every quarter?

During the ABN registration process, and if you're registering for GST, there are some choices to make. Firstly, do you want to report on cash or accruals? "Cash" means you only have to report on the GST on customer payments that you have received and business expenses that have been physically paid.

"Accrual" means you have to report on all customer income, even if you haven't been paid yet (customers that have outstanding amounts with you) and you can claim all expenses including ones that you haven't paid yet, so purchases that you have put on an account. For most small businesses, the easiest way to report GST is on a cash basis so you don't have to worry about paying GST you haven't yet got the cash in your hand.

The last choice on the GST registration form is whether you want to report quarterly, monthly or annually. If your turnover is more than $20 million you must report monthly, but for the purposes of this book, you wouldn't then be a small business!

Most businesses must report quarterly, and the annual option is only available if you voluntarily registered for GST – that is, your turnover is less than $75,000. You can elect to report monthly and some businesses see this as a good way to keep on top of their GST obligations. While this might seem like a great idea, there are some negatives.

Firstly you must report and pay your GST by the twenty first day of the following month, three weeks after the months' end. That is a very short period to pay! The other negative is that there are no extensions.

Quarterly activity statements are due on the twenty-eighth day of the month following the end of the quarter. The Business Activity Statement covering April 1 to the June 30 would be due to be lodged and paid on the July 28.

The secret here is that tax agents have an extra three weeks to lodge and that means you get extra time to pay. The only time it doesn't apply is for the quarter ending December 31, which is due on the February 28.

The biggest issue with being registered for GST and having to do a BAS is making sure you keep on top of them. Refer back to record keeping for how to do this. If you lodge a BAS (or any other tax document for that matter) late, the ATO can fine you $170 per 28 days or part thereof to a maximum of $850 if you are a small entity. But if your turnover is greater than $1 million then the penalty is doubled. To make matters worse, this penalty isn't tax deductible!

The ATO will also impose a General Interest Charge (GIC) of 9.15% per annum or 0.0235% per day on unpaid amounts owing to them. This interest is deductible but still, it's a huge whack to the bank account.

If you have employees you will also need to register for PAYG withholding. Remember, if you are running your business through a company or a trust, you yourself might be an employee. Wages and PAYG withholding are reported on your business activity statements quarterly unless your total PAYG withholding is greater than $25,000. If that's the case, you will have to report and PAYG withholding monthly.

Unpaid PAYG withholding is something the ATO can pursue company directors for personally.

In Australia, GST is usually $1/11^{th}$ of the price of the goods or services, so something that is advertised at a $1.10 would include 10c of GST. Once you are registered for GST you have to add it to all goods or services you provide, unless they are considered GST free.

Things that are GST free include these categories (among others):

- Fresh food
- Medical services
- Education
- Child care
- Medicines
- Exported goods and services

If the goods or services you are selling are GST free you can still claim the GST for the business expenses you have.

Income tax is messy and complicated. Our tax system is based on the Income Tax Assessment Act 1936, Income Tax Assessment Act 1997, associated regulations, tax rulings and case law. It's a lot of information to understand. Unless your business is as a tax agent, there is no way you are going to get your head around it all.

The most important thing I can say is, don't listen to your friends' advice – unless they are a tax agent!

It's amazing how much car park and water cooler gossip goes around about what can be claimed. I had a client tell me her friend had said she could claim her bras as her job required physical labour and they needed super supportive underwear! I had to say no. The main rule as to whether something is claimable or not is that it must have a direct connection to the income you are generating – or trying to generate.

There are also certain categories of things that aren't claimable or have to be claimed over a number of years – referred to as "depreciated". Fines and penalties are not claimable, and neither are entertainment expenses (in some circumstances – you'd have to be a movie reviewer to do so).

It can also be confusing as to what you can claim if you finance equipment. In most cases, it's the interest on the finance (not the repayments) that you can claim, as well as the depreciation on the equipment. The only exception is if you have a lease agreement –

then the repayments are the claimable amount and nothing else.

Regardless of what sort of entity you operate, the profit of the business is calculated on the assessable income – what you charge your customers, less GST, less the allowable deductions, which are your expenses less the GST. This profit is what the ATO calls the business' assessable income and what they charge tax against. At what rate the business profit is taxed depends on how your business is structured.

As an example, let's say Widgets and Wodgets (W&W) Transport made a profit of $100,000 for the 2014 year.

If W&W were a sole trader, then this profit would be added to any other income the owner might have and would be taxed at the marginal rate plus Medicare levy and surcharges if applicable. So if this was the only income the owner had and they had no kids or private health insurance they would pay $27,447. This would be an effective tax rate of 27.4%.

If W&W operated through a partnership that was a 50/50 split then the taxable income would be $50,000 each. Assuming that each partner has no other income, no kids and no health insurance, each partner would pay $8,297 each – an effective tax rate of 16.6%.

If W&W operated through a company, it would be taxed at a flat rate of 30% –$30,000 in income tax.

And if it operated through a trust, the tax could be anything – it would depend on how much was distributed to each beneficiary.

While tax planning should be part of the consideration of what structure to operate under, it shouldn't be the overwhelming choice. Re-read the "Set up for Success" section to remind you of the other things that need to be considered.

Although there is no legal obligation to get your tax prepared by a tax agent, it is definitely money well spent to ensure it's done correctly. If the ATO performs an audit and finds you've stuffed up, the penalties can be high. If they think you've been careless they can sting you an extra 49% in tax as a penalty. Even if the ATO decides it was an honest mistake, they will still charge interest on the amount that needs to be paid after the outcome of the audit.

If a tax agent advises you and then prepares your return, and they can show that you relied on them, then there are "safe harbour" provisions to prevent you from being penalised.

The other thing worth considering is audit insurance. This is relatively inexpensive – about $500 per year. What it covers is your tax agent's time in dealing with an audit. Most tax agents will charge anywhere from about $150-500 per hour depending on their level of expertise.

If you think a basic audit is likely to take a couple of hours, you'd be wrong. On average, most will take about four to six hours, so you can see that audit insurance is worth it.

Tax is a very complex area and the examples I've given here are deliberately broad. It is essential you seek advice specific to your circumstances before making any decisions.

Succession planning

Nobody wants to die at their desk and for most of us the idea of life is to work to live, not the other way around. So how do you get out of your business while taking the maximum value you can? What are your options?

The obvious one is to sell to a completely independent party and this is where the best value is likely to be found. Another option commonly seen in small business is a transfer to the next generation. The problem with this is that you still have to eat!

Most importantly, what happens to your business if you can no longer run it, either through illness or because you've shuffled off to heaven? What happens to what might be one of your biggest assets?

All this comes back to planning and it is planning that should start at the beginning of your business. It is important to set down your future goals and this can be part of your business plan in the "About the Future" section.

Obviously, over the time your business is in operation, your circumstances can change – marriages begin, children are born, divorces happen. It's important that your succession plan is reviewed and revised.

Part of making succession easy is getting the setup of the entity right in the first place, making sure you have shareholders and partnership agreements in place. Buy/sell agreements are also important, as is life insurance. Allison and I have policies on each other so that if one of us falls off the perch, the other can pay out the deceased's family and still have funds to hire a replacement.

This is an area where it is essential to seek legal advice. As part of a strong succession plan, it is important to have a current will and powers of attorney in place. It's also necessary to work with your accountant to determine how the business would be valued for your estate. A financial planner is also a good person to add to the mix as we will see in the next section. Retirement is the flow-on of succession planning.

Unfortunately death is unavoidable, but hopefully we all get to retire first!

Retirement

Ahhh, the golden years!

My generation has to suck it up a bit longer than my parents'. We can't access our super until 60 and there will be no aged pension until 70 so what happens if I'm ready to become a grey nomad at 55 – what are my choices?

So, you've now been operating your business successfully for fifteen years and you're ready to dance off into the sunset. You have a business plan and succession plan and you know that to retire early you need to sell your business for the maximum you can and minimise any tax consequences.

When you sell a business, another type of tax raises its ugly head. It's called Capital Gains Tax. This one also applies when you sell investments, including property. What is taxed in this case is the profit or gain you've made on the business. Luckily the government understands that for many small businesses much of their retirement planning is tied up in their business value and so graciously provides some capital gains tax concessions. The best one is if your business classifies as small business, you are over 55, and you've owned the business for at least 15 years – if this is the case, you don't pay Capital Gains Tax. Woohoo!

This is why succession planning is so important. You're 54 and have had the business for 15 years. You've had enough and want to get out. It may be best to hang in until you're 55 to take advantage of the tax savings.

When it comes to retirement, it is not just your accountant you need, unless your accountant is also a certified financial planner. A good financial planner needs to be involved well before you decide to retire. They can help you plan for retirement, work out how best to structure things like superannuation and business sales, to achieve the best retirement funds possible. They can also help you in the lead up to retirement by looking at how your super is invested and how to maximise it. The other thing to consider is how to balance it all so you are eligible for some aged pension as well. After all, you've had a successful business – and have dutifully paid your taxes – for years.

Your accountant is still important in this area as they know your tax position and the value and workings of your business. A good relationship between the financial planner and your accountant will also make the move to retirement much smoother.

CHAPTER FIVE
GO FORTH AND PROSPER

Over the course of this book, we've gone from start to finish. While it's not comprehensive, hopefully it's given you a starting point in developing, maintaining and selling a successful business.

To recap:

- Plan to do – planning is important all through your business life. Remember to research, review and revise.

- Set up for success – get the structure and the record keeping right from the start.

- People who need people – people are the most important aspect of your business. We are all humans. Respect each other and choose wisely.

- Death and taxes – both are unavoidable so make sure you plan for both.

- Retirement – make the most of all your hard work by getting the right help to set up for retirement before you even serve your first customer.

I hope you got something from this book. There are oodles of resources for planning, as well as really helpful templates, on the internet. I haven't included any here – just use your favourite search engine.

Just like people, each business is unique and individual. Embrace that individuality, always be yourself, and aim high.

Now, go forth and prosper!

Kathryn Harris

www.ingramcontent.com/pod-product-compliance
Lightning Source LLC
Chambersburg PA
CBHW060641210326
41520CB00010B/1691